The Little
Black Book of
Retirement
Wisdom

Amusing Quotes for Retirees

Mike Kowis, Esq.

THE LITTLE BLACK BOOK OF RETIREMENT WISDOM:

Amusing Quotes for Retirees

by Mike Kowis, Esq.

Library of Congress Control Number: 2024903245

ISBN-13: 979-8-9900133-1-5 (paperback)

ISBN-13: 979-8-9900133-0-8 (eBook)

www.mikekowis.com

Lecture PRO Publishing

Conroe, Texas

Dedication

This book is dedicated to those who hung up their work boots after a long and successful career. May God bless all retirees with new adventures and no alarm clocks!

Testimonials

Here's what people are saying about *The Little Black Book of Retirement Wisdom*:

This book does for retirees what screen doors did for submarines. – *Mayor of Kenefick, Texas*

Shouldn't this book be printed in LARGE FONT? – *Mike's eye doctor*

What does Mike know about retirement? He thought AARP stood for American Association of Retiree Pickleball. – *Mike's personal masseuse*

I'm not saying Mike's new book is a waste of time, but he put the pro in unproductive. – *Mike's neighbor*

Another quote book from Mike? It's as if *The Little Black Book of Tax Wisdom* wasn't embarrassing enough. – *Mike's literary agent*

***The Little Black Book of Retirement Wisdom* is AWESOME... for squashing mosquitos!** – *Grandpa Kowis*

Mike should write more books using the words of other people. – *Mike's high school principal*

Just when I thought Mike finally turned his life around, he releases this dumpster fire. – *the local bartender*

The title of this book contains the word "little," but that's not the only thing little about Mike. – *Mike's investment banker*

But seriously, you're gonna enjoy the following collection of amusing retirement quotes. Let's just hope they don't make you want to retire from reading as much as the silly testimonials above!

Contents

INTRODUCTION

> **Retirement is when you stop living at**
> **work and start working at living.**
> — *Unknown*

FIFTY THOUSAND HOURS! That's how long I've spent grinding away at my desk during the last twenty-five years (40 hours per week X 50 weeks per year X 25 years = 50,000 hours). Celebrating this work anniversary made me think about the days ahead, including my golden years.

Ah, sweet retirement. What will that be like? Will I relish every moment of freedom or feel bored and unfulfilled? Shall I commit my life to new passions or watch the lazy days pass from the comfort of my easy chair. Will my hard-earned nest egg support me until I croak or will I end up dining on dog food during my last moments on earth? We all grapple with these burning questions if we are lucky enough to reach this stage of life. To anyone contemplating the "Big R," take heart! You might find some of the answers in this silly book filled with 501 humorous and thought-provoking quotes about retirement.

The quotations below touch on a wide variety of concepts related to life after work, including well-known sayings, quips, financial advice, religious teachings, and much more. Each chapter covers a different topic, but there is a degree of overlap.

Following this Introduction, Chapters 1 through 3 include famous sayings, humorous quotes, and the true meaning of retirement, respectively. In addition to Chapter 2, you'll find funny quips sprinkled throughout the entire book.

Chapter 4 recommends acquiring a new purpose in life, and Chapter 5 explores the joy of personal freedom provided by retirement. Next, Chapters 6 and 7 explain the importance of saving a nest egg and the concept that your golden years should be viewed as a second childhood, respectively.

Chapters 8 and 9 discuss the morbid view that retirement equals death and spiritual advice related to retirement, respectively. On a lighter note, Chapter 10 shares personal reasons for deciding to permanently exit the workforce and the timing thereof.

Chapter 11 confesses deep regret felt by some folks regarding their retirement decision, while Chapter 12 describes the notion that retirement is never an option. Next, Chapter 13 discusses retirement for celebrities, artists, and professional athletes. Chapter 14 includes sayings that didn't fit neatly elsewhere. Finally, the Conclusion distills the below quotations into a handful of salient points and shares my top ten list.

I hope you enjoy the following retirement quotes as much as I enjoyed gathering them. Happy reading – and you can quote me on that!

CHAPTER 1

Famous Sayings

> **Retire from work, but not from life.**
> — *M.K. Soni*

And in the end, it's not the years in your life that count. It's the life in your years.

— *President Abraham Lincoln*

Retirement: That's when you return from work one day and say, "Hi, Honey, I'm home – forever."

— *Gene Perret*

What do you call a person who is happy on a Monday? Retired.

— *Unknown*

Half our life is spent trying to find something to do with the time we have rushed through life trying to save.

— *Will Rogers*

Retirement: When you stop lying about your age and start lying around the house.

— *Unknown*

Retirement enables you to trade your stress-induced wrinkles for laughter lines and experience the joy of aging gracefully.

— *David Wilson, Retire and Rejuvenate (2013)*

We all retire one day. If we want to, if we don't want to.

— *Donatella Versace*

Life begins at retirement.

— *Unknown*

Often when you think you are at the end of something, you're at the beginning of something else.

— *Fred Rogers*

Retirement: World's longest coffee break.

— *Unknown*

Retiring young isn't for everybody, even if you think it is. When all you have is a hammer, everything looks like a nail.

— *Pat Cadigan*

Retirement is a blank sheet of paper. It is a chance to redesign your life into something new and different.

— *Patrick Foley, Winning at Retirement: A Guide to Health, Wealth & Purpose in the Best Years of Your Life (2022)*

When a man retires and time is no longer a matter of urgent importance, his colleagues generally present him with a watch.

— *R.C. Sheriff*

I will never retire. I'm going to die with my boots on.

— *Walter Mercado*

Age is an issue of mind over matter. If you don't mind, it doesn't matter.

— *Mark Twain*

The trouble with retirement is that you never get a day off.

— *Abe Lemons*

Retiring is one thing. Being retired is something else altogether.

— *Mike Wallace, Between You and Me: A Memoir (2005)*

When I retire, I'm going to spend my evenings by the fireplace going through those boxes. There are things in there that ought to be burned.

— *President Richard M. Nixon*

Retirement itself is the best gift. No gold watch could ever top it.

— *Abigail Charleson*

Retirement is not the end of the road. It is the beginning of the open highway.

— *Unknown*

If people concentrated on the really important things in life, there'd be a shortage of fishing poles.

— *Doug Larson*

In retirement, every day is Boss's Day and every day is Employee Appreciation Day.

  – *Terri Guillemets*

A grand adventure is about to begin.

  – *Winnie-the-Pooh*

CHAPTER 2

Wisecracks

> **My parents didn't want to move to Florida,**
> **but they turned sixty and that's the law.**
> — *Jerry Seinfeld*

When a man retires, his wife gets twice as much husband for half as much money.

— *Chi Chi Rodriguez*

In my retirement I go for a short swim at least once or twice every day. It's either that or buy a new golf ball.

— *Gene Perret*

Retirement is like sex. Men love to talk about it, but when the time finally comes they're good for about fifteen minutes. Then they're dying to put their ties back on.

— *Paula Wall*

The biggest challenge of retirement is how to drink coffee without getting it on your pajamas.

— *Unknown*

A latte a day keeps retirement away.

— *David Bach*

Ah, blissful retirement. With the company's stocks down, I'll finally enjoy some prime moments with my couch.

— *Homer Simpson, The Simpsons*

I'm going to retire hopefully like Cary Grant did. I'll be on stage telling a story, everyone's going to applaud and laugh, and then I'll drop like a rock.

— *Burt Reynolds*

Asked once what he was doing to keep busy in retirement, Hank Aaron replied, "I'm being Hank Aaron."

— *Jane Leavy, Sandy Koufax: A Lefty's Legacy (2002)*

I can't wait to retire so I can get up at 6 o'clock in the morning and go drive around really slow and make everybody late for work.

— *Unknown*

Retirement means no pressure, no stress, no heartache… unless you play golf.

— *Gene Perret*

Working people have a lot of bad habits, but the worst of these is work.

— *Clarence Darrow*

When some people retire, it's going to be mighty hard to be able to tell the difference.

— *Virginia Graham*

There's one thing I always wanted to do before I quit… retire!

— *Groucho Marx*

Retirement is the time when you never do all the things you intended to do when you were still working.

— *Earl Wilson*

The money's no better in retirement, but the hours are.

— *Unknown*

The best thing about retirement is not having to wear pants.

  – Mark Hewer

You know you are getting old when everyone else looks young.

  – Steven Magee

Retirement is having nothing to do and someone always keeping you from it.

  – Robert Brault

Four months ago, he had a mild heart attack and his doctor told him to retire. He found another doctor.

  – John Grisham, Rogue Lawyer (2015)

If your monthly income exceeds your lifestyle expenses including taxes, guess what? You're retired!

  – M.J. DeMarco, The Millionaire Fastlane: Crack the Code to Wealth and Live Rich for a Lifetime! (2010)

Sugar Ray Leonard's retirements last about as long as Elizabeth Taylor's marriages.

  – Bob Arum

Instead of saving for someone else's college education, I'm currently saving for a luxury retirement community replete with golf carts and handsome young male nurses who love butterscotch.

— *Jen Kirkman*

Retirement at sixty-five is ridiculous. When I was sixty-five, I still had pimples.

— *George Burns*

My dad's the type that would die six months after retiring, so I plan to have him work here forever.

— *Rick Harrison, Pawn Stars Interview*

Retired is being tired twice, I've thought, first tired of working, then tired of not.

— *Richard Armour*

He who laughs last at the boss's jokes probably isn't far from retirement.

— *Unknown*

The company accountant is shy and retiring. He's shy a quarter-million dollars. That's why he's retiring.

— *Milton Berle*

I'm what you might call retired. It's a refined name for bum.

    — Danny McGuire, Xanadu (1980)

I don't think you retire from movies; movies retire you.

    — Michael Caine

The company gave me an aptitude test and I found out the work I was best suited for was retirement.

    — Unknown

How has retirement affected my golf game? A lot more people beat me now.

    — President Dwight D. Eisenhower

What do gardeners do when they retire?

    — Bob Monkhouse

The car provided Americans with an enviable standard of living. You could not get a steady job with high wages and health and retirement benefits working on the General Livestock Corporation assembly line putting udders on cows.

    — P.J. O'Rourke

I figure the faster I pedal, the faster I can retire.

– Lance Armstrong

I was voted Most Likely to Make a Teacher Retire.

– Russ

Golf is played by twenty million mature American men whose wives think they are out having fun.

– Jim Bishop

Retirement is wonderful. It's doing nothing without worrying about getting caught at it.

– Gene Perret

When men reach their sixties and retire, they go to pieces. Women go right on cooking.

– Gail Sheehy

Maybe wanting to retire is my ambition.

– Brenda Blethyn

I'm not just retiring from the company; I'm also retiring from my stress, my commute, my alarm clock, and my iron.

– *Hartman Jule*

You have to retire before you can make the Hall of Fame.

– *Joe Garagiola*

You're starting to see a lot of fighters like, "We want more money so we can be able to retire eventually," instead of we get to 30 years old and we're like, "Alright, I think Costco has openings."

– *Demetrious Johnson*

Retirement is like a never-ending weekend party, except you can't recover with a day off on Monday.

– *Margaret Johnson, Retirement Bliss (2009)*

Retirement is waking up in the morning with nothing to do and by bedtime having done only half of it.

– *Anonymous*

Retirement isn't so bad. Give me a tall drink, a plush sofa and a rerun of *Matlock*, and you can have the rest. Matlock is my hero. He never loses.

– *Ken Venturi*

I had a very detailed retirement plan, and I feel like I've met every aspect of it: a lot of golf, a lot of carbs, a lot of fried food, and some booze, occasionally - I've been completely committed... The results have shown.

— *Andy Roddick*

When you retire, you switch bosses. From the one who hired you to the one who married you.

— *Gene Perret*

CHAPTER 3

By Definition

> **Retirement is a journey, not a destination.**
> — *Rick Steves*

Retirement is the state of being able to afford to do things that you have always wanted to do, but are now too old to even think about doing.

— *Ivan Cotter*

Retirement is not the end of the world. It is the beginning of understanding that life isn't only about work.

— *Unknown*

Retirement is when having a good time is the only thing on your to do list.

— *Robert Brault*

Retirement is a ticket to endless vacation.

— *Unknown*

To me, retirement means doing what you have fun doing.

— *Dick Van Dyke*

Retirement is a time to enjoy the fruits of your labor.

— *Unknown*

Retirement is the ugliest word in the language.

— *Ernest Hemingway*

Retirement in America has come to mean "save enough money so I can quit the job I hate."

— *Anonymous*

Retirement is not about "stopping." It's about pausing enough to let your soul catch up.

— *Unknown*

Retirement is not the finish line; it is the new beginning. Retirement is not your last paragraph; it is the long, rich, rewarding final chapters of your own book – as many pages as you can dream up. Retirement is not the end of your life; it is the beginning of the best years of your life!

> – *Chris Hogan, Retire Inspired: It's Not an Age, It's a Financial Number (2016)*

Retirement is the beginning of a whole new life.

> – *Marianna Malthouse, Tanya (2014)*

That's what retirement's for, isn't it? Doing the things you always wanted to do but never dared.

> – *Marianne Cronin, The One Hundred Years of Lenni and Margot (2021)*

For retirement brings repose, and repose allows a kindly judgement of all things.

> – *U.S. Senator John Sharp Williams*

Retirement is a time to be grateful for the blessings of the past and the opportunities of the future.

> – *Unknown*

Retiring is the easy way out.

— *Venus Williams*

Retirement is a stage where an employer discards an employee that he cannot exploit further.

— *Mokokoma Mokhonoana*

Retirement: When you have an income without a job and a life without a boss.

— *Unknown*

Retirement Systemization: The whole point of being financially free is that you don't actually need to do any work.

— *George Choy, RETIRE NOW! Your Blueprint to Financial Freedom Through Property (2019)*

Remember, what does "retirement" mean? It doesn't mean that you're a couch potato. Leisure is not the same thing as rest. If you're bicycling five miles a day, that's leisure, but it certainly takes a lot of effort.

— *Robert Fogel*

Retirement isn't the end of work. It's the end of mandatory work.

— *Mr. Money Mustache*

Retired just means I don't have a job description, and I can work on what I want now.

— *Dennis E. Taylor, Heaven's River (2020)*

Retirement is when life begins to present itself in technicolor instead of black and white.

— *Laura Thompson, Embracing Retirement (2017)*

Retirement is when you realize that laughing at yourself is far more entertaining than being serious all the time.

— *William Thompson, Jokes and Wisdom for Retirees (2007)*

CHAPTER 4

New Purpose

> **Don't simply retire from something;**
> **have something to retire to.**
> — *Harry Emerson Fosdick*

Retirement is a new beginning, and that means closing the book on one chapter in order to begin the next.

— *Sid Miramontes*

Retirement's greatest challenge isn't surviving financially; it's finding a new purpose.

— *Rob Lowe*

It is now thirteen years since I ceased to accumulate wealth and began to distribute it. I could never have succeeded in either had I stopped with having enough to retire upon, but nothing to retire to.

— *Andrew Carnegie, The Autobiography of Andrew Carnegie and the Gospel of Wealth (2006)*

If retirement means laying on a beach and rubbing cocoa butter on your stomach, about 48 hours of that will be enough for most people. You'll want something new.

    — *Tim Ferriss*

You have said that your most important final message is to "live life in crescendo." What does that mean? It means that the most important work you will ever do is always ahead of you. It is never behind you. You should always be expanding and deepening your commitment to that work. Retirement is a false concept. You may retire from a job, but never from meaningful projects and contributions.

    — *Stephen R. Covey, The 7 Habits of Highly Effective People (1989)*

Retirement gives you the time literally to recreate yourself through a sport, game or hobby that you always wanted to try or that you haven't done in years.

    — *Steven D. Price*

To me, the unhappiest people in the world are those in the watering places, the international watering places like... uh... the south coast of France and Newport and Palm Springs and Palm Beach; going to parties every night, playing golf every afternoon, then bridge. Drinking too much, talking too much, thinking too little. Retired. No purpose.

    — *President Richard M. Nixon*

It is never too late to be what you might have been.

— *George Eliot*

Now is your time. Go for it! It is never too late, or too early, to begin living the adventures of which you have always dreamed.

— *Patricia Reid-Waugh, Retirement: A New Adventure (2016)*

I've been talking about retiring for years. It's my standard answer to the question, "What are your future plans?" The truth is, I'll always want to do things that are worthwhile or fun.

— *Dick Van Dyke*

You are never too old to set a new goal or dream a new dream.

— *C.S. Lewis*

Dare to live the life you have dreamed for yourself. Go forward and make your dreams come true.

— *Ralph Waldo Emerson*

What does retirement mean now that there are so many opportunities for learning, for caring, for serving? We can redefine aging.

— *Rachel Cowan*

I will say that when I retire, I will probably do something to help others. I don't know what it will be... probably I'll get involved in some charity.

— *Vanna White*

Planning to retire? Before you do find your hidden passion, do the thing that you have always wanted to do.

— *Catherine Pulsifer*

Retirement is not about being idle. It's about a new adventure, a new journey.

— *Unknown*

Never stop learning. View technology as a means to personal growth, and seek out opportunities to continually learn in your retirement years.

— *Fritz Gilbert, Keys to a Successful Retirement: Staying Happy, Active, and Productive in Your Retired Years (2020)*

Retirement: When you stop working for money and start working for a cause.

— *Unknown*

As in all successful ventures, the foundation of a good retirement is planning.

  – *Earl Nightingale*

For me, being in retirement, it was just having the opportunity to watch other stuff and do different things.

  – *Shawn Michaels*

Retirement is not the end; it is the beginning of a lifelong exploration of who you really are and what truly matters to you.

  – *Emily Wilson, Retire: A Journey of Self-Discovery (2014)*

When our career is over, when we retire and the basketball stops bouncing, we still have to find something else to do.

  – *John Wall*

There is a whole new kind of life ahead, full of experiences just waiting to happen. Some call it retirement. I call it bliss.

  – *Betty Sullivan*

I see retirement as just another of these reinventions, another chance to do new things and be a new version of myself.

  – *Walt Mossberg*

Retirement is the perfect time to pack your bags and follow your dreams.

— *Unknown*

Retirement is not a time to sit back; it's a time to move forward, to explore new horizons and discover new passions.

— *Dennis Waitley*

Retirement isn't the end of the road, but just a turn in the road.

— *Unknown*

I doubt I'll ever retire, but if I do, I see myself as the little old Parisian lady pushing her trolley from the supermarket to her apartment. Everyone needs a pipe dream.

— *Catherine Martin*

Retirement is the time to fling open the windows of your mind and let the fresh air of new experiences fill your soul.

— *Robert Johnson, A New Chapter: The Art of Retiring Well (2008)*

You don't retire from a job (which may have become stale), but to an activity that is meaningful to you.

— *Viktor E. Frankl, Recollections: An Autobiography (1995)*

After retiring, I was a little bored with nothing to do and got fat. I thought, if a 60-year-old metabolic fat man, after five years, can get to Mount Everest, that would be very exciting.

— *Yuichiro Miura*

Preparation for old age should begin not later than one's teens. A life which is empty of purpose until 65 will not suddenly become filled on retirement.

— *Dwight L. Moody*

Retirement is not a life without purpose; it is the ongoing purpose that provides meaningfulness.

— *Robert Rivers*

CHAPTER 5

Freedom

> **For many, retirement is a time for personal growth,**
> **which becomes the path to greater freedom.**
> — *Robert Delamontagne*

Retirement is the grandest ticket to freedom — freedom to explore, freedom to discover. Pack your bags and go.

— *Unknown*

There's never enough time to do all the nothing you want.

— *Bill Watterson*

Retirement: A time to do what you want to do, when you want to do it, where you want to do it, and how you want to do it.

— *Catherine Pulsifer*

Retirement is the time to open a new chapter in your life story. You decide what's next!

— Unknown

Retirement is the ultimate life hack. You get to escape the monotonous routine of work and embrace the freedom to indulge in your passions.

— John Smith, The Joy of Retirement (2015)

Retirement: A time to enjoy all the things you never had time to do when you worked.

— Catherine Pulsifer

We work all our lives so we can retire — so we can do what we want with our time — and the way we define or spend our time defines who we are and what we value.

— Bruce Linton

After I retire, for some time at least, I will spend my time with my grandchildren and my family members, because all these years, 50 years, I have not been able to give my time to them.

— India President Pratibha Patil

Retirement is when the workaholic finally learns to chill and appreciate the simple pleasures life has to offer.

   — Daniel Martin, The Workaholic's Guide to Retirement (2011)

Retirement means doing whatever I want to do. It means choice.

   — Dianne Nahirny

I enjoy waking up and not having to go to work. So, I do it three or four times a day.

   — Gene Perret

Retirement is the opportunity to laugh at yourself, enjoy life's quirks, and appreciate the absurdities that come your way.

   — Sandra Collins, Retire and Unwind (2019)

Retirement is an opportunity to explore the highest peaks and the deepest valleys without worrying about the clock.

   — Unknown

In retirement, every day is Saturday. It's like having a permanent weekend, full of relaxation and leisure.

   — Michael Anderson, Living the Dream: Retire and Thrive (2012)

People can't do anything about growing older because it's one of the most natural things in the world. But one thing you can control, though, is how you'll live your life once you're old enough to retire.

    – Adrian J. Williams

I am looking forward to retiring, or at least having more time. When I was young, I wanted more stuff. Now I am older, I want more time.

    – Richard Coles

I enjoy being active, but I look forward to the day when I can retire to the Internet.

    – Daniel Kahneman

CHAPTER 6

Nest Egg

> **Say goodbye to tension and hello to your pension.**
> — *Unknown*

If you put nothing away for retirement, I can tell you, to the last penny, how much you will have when you retire: nothing.

— *John C. Bogle*

Retirement is like a long vacation in Las Vegas. The goal is to enjoy it to the fullest, but not so fully that you run out of money.

— *Jonathan Clements*

My retirement plan is to get thrown into a minimum-security prison in Hawaii.

— *Julius Sharpe*

Going through chemo is like investing money in a retirement account. You feel the hit right now, but later in life you get to reap the benefits - by still being alive.

— *Regina Brett*

Money is something you got to make in case you don't die.

— *Max Asnas*

Anyone with a pension or retirement is an investor in the stock market.

— *Brad Katsuyama*

The key to a happy retirement is to have enough money to live on, but not enough to worry about.

— *Unknown*

According to the Social Security Administration, if you take any 100 people at the start of their working careers and follow them for the next 40 years until they reach retirement age, here's what you'll find: only 1 will be wealthy; 4 will be financially secure; 5 will continue working, not because they want to but because they have to; 36 will be dead; and 54 will be broke and dependent on friends, family, relatives, and the government to take care of them.

— *Hal Elrod, The Miracle Morning: The Not-So-Obvious Secret Guaranteed to Transform Your Life: Before 8AM (2012)*

I am a Georgia guy, and I have Brett Favre's card when he played with the Atlanta Falcons. That's my retirement plan.

— *Forrest Griffin*

Retirement: It's nice to get out of the rat race, but you have to learn to get along with less cheese.

— *Gene Perret*

Retirement is when you stop sacrificing today for an imaginary tomorrow.

— *Eric Jorgenson, The Almanac of the Naval Ravikant: A Guide to Wealth and Happiness (2020)*

The longer you work, the more money you'll have for retirement. But the longer you work, the less time you'll have to enjoy that retirement.

— *Wall Street Journal*

For many people, being asked to solve their own retirement savings problems is like being asked to build their own cars.

— *Richard Thaler*

Sadly, retirement planning, in many circumstances, has become nothing more than planned procrastination.

— *Richie Norton, The Power of Starting Something Stupid (2012)*

You can be young without money, but you can't be old without it.

— *Tennessee Williams*

To enjoy a long, comfortable retirement, save more today.

— *Suze Orman*

Saving money is good. Saving dreams is not good.

— *Richie Norton*

If your retirement plan is to win the lottery, you will have to work forever as a greeter at the local shopping center and eat cat food for supper.

— *Steve Repak, Dollars & Uncommon Sense: Basic Training for Your Money (2011)*

Before you speak, listen. Before you write, think. Before you spend, earn. Before you invest, investigate. Before you criticize, wait. Before you pray, forgive. Before you quit, try. Before you retire, save. Before you die, give.

— *William Arthur Ward*

If you don't like the idea that most of the money spent on lottery tickets supports government programs, you should know that most of the earnings from mutual funds support investment advisors' and mutual fund managers' retirement.

    — *Robert Kiyosaki*

My guiding principle and motivation was that I wanted to retire by the time I turned 35. There actually are two books that I bought and still have - Paul Terhost's *Cashing In On the American Dream: How to Retire at 35* and Andrew Tobias's *The Only Investment Guide You'll Ever Need* - that were my personal financial road map.

    — *Mark Cuban*

The rate of return on Social Security for people nearing retirement is about 1.5 percent. By the time young children like mine are ready to retire, that rate of return will be a negative percentage.

    — *U.S. Representative Paul Ryan*

Social security was never intended to be a retirement plan. At most, it was designed to provide an income supplement.

    — *David Bach, Smart Women Finish Rich: 9 Steps to Achieving Financial Security and Funding Your Dreams*

Social Security and Medicare were sold to the public as insurance programs. They are not. As such, they now rely mostly on the "contributions" of younger workers and massive federal borrowing to subsidize them. Despite repeated and dire warnings about their unsustainable fiscal condition from the trustees appointed to oversee them, younger workers are compelled to continue to pay into these programs, from which they are unlikely to benefit upon their retirement and for which future generations will bear the brunt of their eventual collapse.

— Mark R. Levin, Plunder and Deceit: Big Government's Exploitation of Young People and the Future (2015)

The main purpose of Social Security is to redistribute wealth, to make an increasingly large number of Americans dependent on government for their basic needs in their retirement years.

— Neal Boortz

There are basically two ways to help people get sufficient money to fund their entire retirement. The first is to get people to save more money, and to start saving at a younger age. The second approach is to get people to die at a younger age. The easier approach, by far, is getting people to die younger. And how might we achieve this? By allowing citizens to smoke. By subsidizing sugary and fatty foods. By limiting access to preventive health care etc. When we think about retirement savings in these terms, it seems that we're already doing the most we can on this front.

— Dan Ariely, Irrationally Yours: On Missing Socks, Pickup Lines, and Other Existential Puzzles (2015)

My parents and friends, they're Ph.D.s that worked as custodians, that owned their own businesses, that went bankrupt, that moved seven times, that sent their kid to Harvard, that don't have any money for retirement. Highs and lows of life.

— *Roy Choi*

Cessation of work is not accompanied by cessation of expenses.

— *Cato the Elder*

Raising the traditional and early retirement ages will mean extending workers' taxable earning years, fueling economic growth and putting a dent in our unfunded-liabilities crisis by delaying payouts.

— *Michelle Malkin*

Social Security not only helps Americans enjoy a secure retirement, it has also kept millions of Americans out of poverty.

— *U.S. Representative Zoe Lofgren*

People just haven't saved enough for retirement. And they're going to outlive their money.

— *Sallie Krawcheck*

Without Social Security benefits, more than 40 percent of Americans 65 years and older would live below the federal poverty line. Even more striking is that Social Security is the only source of retirement income for almost a quarter of elderly beneficiaries.

— *U.S. Representative Mike Quigley*

We know what's in our Cheerios and in our retirement accounts because the law requires disclosure.

— *Barton Gellman*

A 401(k) is essentially a basket of mutual funds intended to help people save for retirement.

— *Mary Pilon*

Thy shalt not worship thy investment advisor, for if she were so smart she would be retired by now.

— *Steven J. Lee, The Money Plan: Creating Personal Wealth for a Secure Future (2011)*

In money, and in life, you are very often your own worst enemy. You promise yourself you're going to diet, then eat not one or two French fries but a whole plate. You decide to really commit to saving for retirement, only to wind up with a new pair of shoes in your closet.

— *Jean Chatzky*

Real people have trouble balancing their checkbooks, much less calculating how much they need to save for retirement; they sometimes binge on food, drink, or high-definition televisions. They are more like Homer Simpson than Mr. Spock.

– *Richard Thaler*

Our seniors' retirement should never rely on the bull of political promises or the bear of the market.

– *U.S. Senator Barbara Mikulski*

Raising the age of Social Security retirement is not the answer. For so many jobs that are back-breaking jobs, physically burdensome jobs, we're raising the age already to 67. These people are going to struggle to get to that point.

– *U.S. Representative Brad Schneider*

Save when you don't need it, and it'll be there for you when you do.

– *Frank Sonnenberg, The Path to a Meaningful Life (2022)*

While more people are working later in life because of happy things like longer life expectancy, they are also doing so because of very sad things, like a lack of Social Security benefits or retirement plans.

– *Alissa Quart*

We all need to save money to send our kids to college, to buy our first house, and to retire. But the truth is that most of us don't save very much.

— *Timothy Noah*

If I was counselling an individual, and my purpose was to help that individual, the most important thing would be that you should save more. Because don't expect that your retirement will follow those trajectories that some advisers are telling you.

— *Robert J. Shiller*

My instruction to my parents is that I would rather they enjoy their retirement than leave me anything when they go. I am much happier watching them enjoying life.

— *Richard C. Armitage*

It's hard to have any idea of how much money is enough to finance an appropriate lifestyle in retirement. But if a lump sum is translated into a monthly income, it's much easier to determine whether you have enough put away to afford to stop working.

— *Richard Thaler*

As far as your personal goals are and what you actually want to do with your life, it should never have to do with the government. You should never depend on the government for your retirement, your financial security, for anything. If you do, you're screwed.

— *Drew Carey*

Indeed, I think most Americans now know that in 1935 when Social Security was created, there were some 42 Americans working for every American collecting retirement benefits.

— *U.S. Representative John Shadegg*

I'm not sure that too many Americans would choose the president to manage their retirement accounts.

— *U.S. Representative Mike Pompeo*

If Congress wants to mess with the retirement program, why don't we let them start by changing their retirement program, and not have one, instead of talking about getting rid of Social Security and Medicare that was robbed $700 billion dollars to pay for Obamacare.

— *Arkansas Governor Mike Huckabee*

Social Security is the only thing most Americans can count on to keep them out of poverty during retirement.

— *U.S. Representative Ted Deutch*

Retirement security is often compared to a three-legged stool supported by Social Security, employer-provided pension funds, and private savings.

— *U.S. Representative Sander Levin*

Pay off your mortgage before retirement, and that's one less bill you'll have to worry about when you're on a fixed income.

— *Suze Orman*

If you're just starting out in the workforce, the very best thing you can do for yourself is to get started in your workplace retirement plan. Contribute enough to grab any matching dollars your employer is offering (a.k.a. the last free money on earth).

— *Jean Chatzky*

Saving enough to retire has become impossible for most Americans.

— *U.S. Representative Ted Deutch*

Never take a loan against your retirement! When you pay interest against your retirement, you cost yourself interest.

— *Dave Ramsey*

Many people focus on the 4 percent rule, which essentially says that as long as you withdraw no more than 4 percent from your retirement accounts each year, the money should last you 30 years.

— *Jean Chatzky*

A whole generation of Americans will retire in poverty instead of prosperity because they simply are not preparing for retirement now.

— *Scott Cook*

Social Security is not a retirement savings plan; it is a social insurance program. It's a contract that says, as a society, we will look out for you and your family when you can no longer work.

— *U.S. Senator Jeff Bingaman*

Americans used to be able to depend on their jobs to provide a stable retirement.

— *U.S. Representative Keith Ellison*

Automate your savings so that you have money taken directly from each paycheck and deposited into a 401(k) or other workplace retirement account. If that's not an option, automatically have money transferred out of checking into savings each time you get paid.

— *Jean Chatzky*

Retirement: No job, no stress, no pay!

— Unknown

The "aha" moment came one to me one morning when I was applying my mascara, and I realized that the retirement crisis is actually a woman's crisis: Women live longer than men, yet retire with less money.

— Sallie Krawcheck

Retirement is the only time in your life when time no longer equals money.

— Unknown

If you want to retire as a multi-millionaire, then you need to start saving as early as you can.

— John Rampton

Use visual cues to prompt yourself to put away more. A photograph of the beach house where you and your husband can envision spending your retirement will remind you to bump up the contribution to your 401(k).

— Jean Chatzky

Today, more people believe in UFOs than believe that Social Security will take care of their retirement.

— *Scott Cook*

Retirement is having the time to smell the roses, and the money to buy them too.

— *Unknown*

CHAPTER 7

Second Childhood

> **Retirement is the perfect time to embrace your inner child and indulge in the silliness you had to suppress during your working years.**
> *— Linda Thompson, Rediscover your Inner Child: Retirement Edition (2016)*

You can't put off being young until you retire.

— Philip Larkin

Old age is but a second childhood.

— Aristophanes

Retirement is the perfect opportunity to be the class clown once more, letting the laughter of your youth fill the room.

— Laura Davis, Retire and Leave Them Rolling in the Isles (2019)

Don't act your age in retirement. Act like the inner young person you always have been.

— *J.A. West*

Do not grow old, no matter how long you live. Never cease to stand like curious children before the Great Mystery into which we were born.

— *Albert Einstein*

Retirement is when you finally have the time to reconnect with your inner child and embrace your sense of humor without inhibition.

— *Michael Wilson, Laughter and Fulfilment in Retirement (2017)*

Stay young at heart, kind in spirit, and enjoy retirement living.

— *Danielle Duckery*

Retirement's the most wonderful thing. I get to enjoy all the things I never stopped to notice on the way up. After an extraordinary life, it's time to enjoy my retirement.

— *Patrick Macnee*

CHAPTER 8

Dying Wish

Don't you know the quickest way to die is to retire?
— Ralph Ellison, Invisible Man (1952)

Retirement kills more people than hard work ever did.

— *N.J. State Senator Malcolm Forbes*

To "retire" to me means to begin to die. The man who works and is never bored is never old. Work and interest in worthwhile things are the best remedy for age.

— *Pablo Casals*

I think that retirement is the first step towards the grave.

— *Hugh Hefner*

People say, "Are you going to retire?" To me, that sort of equates with lying down and dying. When you're doing something you love to do, why would you stop?

— *Rolf Harris*

I never think about retiring - because you retire, you die.

— *Asha Bhosle*

Energy begets energy. If you are lazy, you will always be lazy. And if you retire at 60, you will die at 65.

— *Dev Anand*

I've seen people get old, retire, and die. Rarely on the same day.

— *Kaulder, The Last Witch Hunter (2015)*

When you retire, you don't get fat and old. C'mon; it's like a shark. Sharks never stop swimming; that's when you die. You gotta keep moving.

— *Reggie Miller*

I think the dirtiest word in the English language is retirement. When you do that, you get old and you get sick and you die.

— *Frank Sinatra, Jr.*

CHAPTER 9

Heavenly Advice

> **Faithful servants never retire. You can retire from your career, but you will never retire from serving God.**
> — *Rick Warren*

I don't even think about a retirement program because I'm working for the Lord, for the Almighty. And even though the Lord's pay isn't very high, his retirement program is, you might say, out of this world.

— *George Foreman*

Retirement is a time to deepen our faith, strengthen our prayers, and be a beacon of God's love to those around us.

— *Joyce Meyer*

Retirement is a time to reflect on God's grace and the journey He has guided us through.

— *Billy Graham*

Retire when your work is done. Such is Heaven's way.

— *Lao Tzu*

I do think Jesus would skip church on Sunday morning and instead visit the nursing homes and retirement homes where so many have abandoned their loved ones.

— *Taylor Negron*

Gray hair is a crown of glory; it is attained in the way of righteousness.

— *Proverbs 16:31, Holy Bible (New International Version)*

I tell people all day who say "When you going to retire?" I said I never found the word retirement in the Bible, so I'm going to keep going till I'm not here.

— *Ted DiBiase, Sr.*

I would challenge anyone to show where God suggests that people should retire.

— *Pat Gelsinger, The Juggling Act: Bringing Balance to Your Faith, Family, and Work (2003)*

The role we have in work may change over time, but the concept of retirement is not biblical.

— *Montana Governor Greg Gianforte*

There are different seasons of life. And there are different callings for different times. The work we do changes over time. But we don't really retire from the work God gives us, we just transition in our calling.

— *Phil Ressler, 40 Things to Give Up for Lent and Beyond: A 40 Day Devotion Series for the Season of Lent (2015)*

I'm banking on my ERA (Eternal Retirement Account) more than my IRA! Do you have an ERA?

— *Evinda Lepins, A Cup of Hope for the Day (2012)*

God never retires his image bearers.

— *Carolyn Curtis James, Half the Church: Recapturing God's Global Vision for Women (2011)*

Other people were looking at my decision in terms of "retirement." I guess that's the right term —retirement – from the NFL, anyway, the only professional career I have ever known. However, I don't think that God ever wants us to retire from relevance or significance. We faced a twofold question: what is the best setting for me to continue to do God's work and how did this fit in with what was best for my family?

— *Tony Dungy, Quiet Strength: The Principles, Practices & Priorities of a Winning Life (2007)*

Retirement is not about slowing down; it's about seeking God's guidance for the next chapter of your life.

— *Joel Olsteen*

A couple took early retirement from their jobs in the Northeast five years ago when he was 59 and she was 51. Now they live in Punta Gorda, Florida, where they cruise on their 30-foot trawler, play softball and collect shells… Picture them before Christ at the great day of judgment: "Look, Lord. See my shells." That is a tragedy.

— *John Piper, Don't Waste Your Life (2003)*

As you step into retirement, trust in God's provision and embrace His plans for your life.

— *T.D. Jakes*

Retirement has never entered my mind for one moment because I don't feel the age I am - and I don't act it, and I don't speak like it. When God calls me, that's when I stop. Until then, I'm going to just keep going.

— *Engelbert Humperdinck*

Retirement is a time to rest in God's goodness and cherish the memories of a well-lived life.

— *Charles Spurgeon*

Retirement is not the goal of a surrendered life, because it competes with God for the primary attention of our lives. Jesus said, "You cannot serve both God and money" and "Wherever your treasure is, your heart will be also."

    – Rick Warren, The Purpose Driven Life: What on Earth Am I Here For? (2002)

God has a plan for your retirement.

    – Billy Graham

In retirement, let God's love and wisdom be the anchors of your soul.

    – Beth Moore

Retirement is a reminder of God's faithfulness throughout your life's journey.

    – Andrew Murray

Retirement is a gift from God, a time to cherish His blessings and serve others with gratitude.

    – Max Lucado

The Lord said to Moses, "This applies to the Levites: Men twenty-five years old or more shall come to take part in the work at the tent of meeting, but at the age of fifty, they must retire from their regular service and work no longer. They may assist their brothers in performing their duties at the tent of meeting, but they themselves must not do the work. This, then, is how you are to assign the responsibilities of the Levites."

– *Numbers 8:23-26, Holy Bible (New International Version)*

CHAPTER 10

Decisions, Decisions

> **How do you know it's time to retire? It's when you stop lying about your age and start bragging about it.**
> — *Unknown*

Don't think of retiring from the world until the world will be sorry that you retire.

— *Samuel Johnson*

The best time to start thinking about your retirement is before the boss does.

— *Unknown*

The question isn't at what age I want to retire, it's at what income.

— *George Foreman*

I just want to retire before I go senile because if I don't retire before I go senile, then I'll do more damage than good at that point.

— *Elon Musk*

Painting was always something I thought I'd do once I retired. But then, about five or six years ago, a good mate passed away suddenly at the age of 50 and it made me realize that if I put off doing stuff until I retire, I might not ever get there.

— *Anh Do*

The harder you work, the harder it is to surrender.

— *Vince Lombardi*

For me, retiring wasn't hard once I knew that that was the decision I was going to make.

— *Gabriela Sabatini*

Why retire from something if you're loving it so much and enjoying it so much, and you're blessed with another group of people to work with like the gang at *Hot in Cleveland*? Why would I think of retiring? What would I do with myself?

— *Betty White*

I wanted to retire on my own terms. I wanted to leave before they kicked me out.

— *Clyde Drexler*

I don't regret the decision to retire. My body was losing its edge. I was taking longer to recover from injuries. You have to get out at some point.

— *David Beckham*

I have two main reasons for retiring. The first is I can no longer play at a level I was accustomed to in the past. That has been very, very frustrating to me throughout this past year. The second one is realizing my health, along with my family, is the most important thing in the world.

— *Mario Lemieux*

As for the reasons behind my retirement, they mostly center around simple fatigue and a fear that if I continue for many more years my work will begin to suffer, or at the very least ease into the yard of mediocre cartoons.

— *Gary Larson*

There will come a time when the public will tire of me and let me know it. That's when I retire. But so far, I've continued to grow. I keep pushing myself to improve.

— *Barbara Mandrell*

It is everyone's prerogative to retire. But it's like giving up on life as far as I'm concerned.

— *Roger Taylor*

Perhaps you should say there should be mandatory retirement even of members of the court, members of the federal judiciary. I'm sure there can be questions about whether one does as good work when you get into your - you know, I'm 67.

— *Supreme Court Chief Justice William Rehnquist*

The time you are happy to sit on the bench, is the time you should retire in my opinion.

— *Adebayo Akinfenwa*

I'm retiring because my time is up.

— *Dave Hickey*

There comes a day when you realize turning the page is the best feeling in the world because you realize there is so much more to the book than the page you were stuck on.

— *Zayn Malik*

I was with Shaq at his home the day he retired. It was innovative for him to become the media and announce via social media that he was retiring.

    – Amy Jo Martin

If you ever think you have all the answers, it's time to retire.

    – Donalyn Miller, The Book Whisperer: Awakening the Inner Reader in Every Child (2009)

There was no last animal I treated. When young farm lads started to help me over the gate into a field or pigpen to make sure the old fellow wouldn't fall, I started to consider retiring.

    – James Herriot

I've decided to pick my moment to retire very carefully – in about 200 years time.

    – Brian Clough

I think that in a year I may retire. I cannot take my money with me when I die and I wish to enjoy it, with my family, while I live. I should prefer living in Germany to any other country, though I am an American, and am loyal to my country.

    – Harry Houdini

I think the day of retirement will come when I go out there and do everything I was supposed to do and I still can't perform. I'm going out there and I'm a danger to myself, then it stresses your family out.

— *Frank Mir*

At the end of your career, you go, "I'm gonna be able to retire undefeated and be one of the very, very few people in history to do it." People were saying I should try and get to 50-0, but my number was 46 - that was it. I could have kept trying, but one loss would have spoiled everything.

— *Joe Calzaghe*

When the butterflies in my stomach, when those leave, then I know it's probably time to retire.

— *Clayton Kershaw*

The day I retire is the day I'll feel old. I'm not there yet.

— *Doug Flutie*

Retiring for good wasn't difficult. I knew at the time it was right. I was no longer capable of achieving the standards I'd set [for] myself and there was no light at the end of the tunnel.

— *Lord Ian Botham*

As a little girl, I said I would retire when I had made my first million. The reality was different. When I did make it, I wanted to make another million, and another, and another after that.

— *Caprice Bourret*

Why go now? That is the question people asked when I announced I was retiring. A combination of things made me feel it was all drawing to a natural end.

— *Graeme Le Saux*

When you stop being nervous is when you should retire. I'm always a little nervous for anything I do because when complacency sets in, that's when I feel it's time to move on to something else.

— *Chris Jericho*

Retiring was scary and it was tough to give up gymnastics, but so many great opportunities have come from it that I never expected.

— *Shawn Johnson*

There's no point in retiring because there's no fun in retiring.

— *Robin Leach*

Sadly, I had to retire from the Bond films. The girls were getting younger, and I was just getting too old.

— *Roger Moore*

I'll know when to retire when I don't want to push myself anymore.

— *Alun Wyn Jones*

There will always be different opinions. Some might argue you should retire after a big success and others that the best time is after a big defeat.

— *Toni Kroos*

When people don't know me anymore or want my autograph, then I'll think about retiring.

— *Johnny Weissmuller*

The positives of retiring outweighed the positives of returning and my desire to still play.

— *Drew Bledsoe*

When a man fell into his anecdotage, it was a sign for him to retire from the world.

— *U.K. Prime Minister Benjamin Disraeli*

Retiring was hard. I'd spent 15 years doing something I loved, but when you get older everything seems to go. When I started spending too long with the physio and the doctor, I knew it was time to call it a day. But I had no preparation for being retired, and I didn't know what to do.

– *Daley Thompson*

I don't really think about retiring. I will retire just before people start saying, "I knew Leonard Slatkin when he conducted well."

– *Leonard Slatkin*

What I'm really looking to do is retire undefeated; I'm not sure when the right time to retire will be, but I know that I'm not done yet. Something still feels unfinished, and that's why I'm going to keep going.

– *Ronda Rousey*

You retire when you are sick and when you can't do it any more or when the public retires you. That's the most painful, because that's the one that leaves you wanting to accomplish more.

– *Julio Iglesias*

Retiring had nothing to do with love of the game. Nothing. It had to do with how I felt about myself. I needed the break.

– *Rolando McClain*

There was a point where there was a vision that we'll get to a certain age, and then we'll retire and be happy. Now that's like, that's being compromised every day. So I think we have to start living happy now and stop waiting for the forty years because by then you'll be so sick, you wouldn't enjoy it anyway.

— *Bruce Lipton*

I always said that when it was time to retire, I would know it, and I would just tip my hat to the crowds.

— *Willie Stargell*

At some point, it comes to an end regardless, however it comes, whether it is retirement or injury; at some point, it comes to an end.

— *Allen Iverson*

In my situation, unlike some players who retire because they have no choice - either teams don't want them or injuries have caused them to retire, and they just can't do it - for me, I really had never thought I would give out mentally before I gave out physically, but I think that was the case.

— *Brett Favre*

If I know I'm at genetically high risk of Alzheimer's, maybe I don't plan to retire at 80, and maybe I'm more proactive about where I'm going to live and who's going to take care of me.

— *Anne Wojcicki*

Boxing's not going to retire me; I'll retire from boxing. That's where most people make mistakes. They normally stay in the game a bit too long.

— *Amir Khan*

Who retires before they even get to the UFC? Losers, that's who.

— *Colby Covington*

CHAPTER 11

Regrets

> **My only regret is that I didn't tell enough people to f*** off.**
> — *Helen Mirren*

I need to retire from retirement.

    — *Supreme Court Justice Sandra Day O'Connor*

Many people take no care of their money till they come nearly to the end of it, and others do just the same with their time.

    — *Johann Wolfgang von Goethe*

I retire for what, like, five minutes, and it all goes to sh*t.

    — *Hawkeye, Captain America: Civil War (2016)*

I wanted to have more time to play and reflect, but I find retirement more stressful than having a nice, steady job because I have to make decisions about where I want to be.

— *Walter Cronkite*

A lot of our friends complain about their retirement. We tell 'em to get a life.

— *Larry Laser*

So, this is retirement? This feeling of emptiness?

— *Zidrou & Aimée de Jongh, The Programmed Obsolescence of Our Feelings (2018)*

I love the game so much. I've been penalized. I've been fined. I have some regrets in my career. But for those four hours on Sunday, you can be free and just let it all go. Retiring had nothing to do with football; it had to do with my family.

— *Randy Moss*

I don't like being retired. It's like announcing an end to your worth, whatever that worth was, and the longer you go on, the more you realize that that worth wasn't worth anything like you once thought it was, and that just makes it worse.

— *Steven Erikson, Toll the Hounds (2008)*

Retirement, to me, is depressing. Depressing.

– *Ben Wallace*

My granny died of cancer she was in her early fifties and in her first year of retirement. It's the cruelest thing and so unfair.

– *Lucy Beaumont*

I feel like some of my peers have a tough time dealing with it and they don't like to talk about retirement.

– *Jim Miller*

I don't think I was a year too late or a year too early in retiring. If the Seahawks had been in the playoffs a year later, I might have had some regrets.

– *U.S. Representative & NFL wide receiver Steve Largent*

I don't want to rush into retirement and regret it, because people say play as long as possible until the legs can't take any more.

– *Phil Neville*

I'm having a really hard time with this retirement thing and not having wrestling.

– *Daniel Bryan*

I never understood that when I heard people retire - they said they missed being around the guys. I don't have a need to make a play in the ninth inning of a game anymore. But being on the inside and being part of a team is something that you really do value and you really do miss.

– *Cal Ripken, Jr.*

I get a lot of letters from people who are really struggling with retirement and getting on each other's nerves.

– *Coleen Nolan*

In 2011, I announced that I was going to retire, and my agent panicked. So she says, "No, no, no. You have to write a book with your husband." My husband is a writer of crime novels. His name is William Gordon. And so I had to accommodate to his style because that's what he writes. So we decided we'd give it a try. Well, we almost divorced.

– *Isabel Allende*

I didn't make enough money in my sport to retire.

– *Roger Staubach*

I wish I hadn't said I'm going to retire.

– *Bradley Wiggins*

How many times have I told them that I'm enjoying life and finally taking my time? While in reality, it's actually time that's taking me, bit by bit, like the cruel tide gnawing at the cliffside. Retirement, my ass! More like a retreat from life!

– *Zidrou & Aimée de Jongh, The Programmed Obsolescence of Our Feelings (2018)*

I haven't quite got the hang of this retirement thing.

– *Walter Cronkite*

In retirement, I have enjoyed it… and everyone misses the game, there's no question, you miss lots of different parts of it.

– *Mike Fisher*

It's one of those things where it's not something you want to do; nobody wants to retire from basketball. You want to play basketball forever. Retirement is admitting to yourself and everybody else that, "I can't do this job anymore." For me, that's not a celebration.

– *Ben Wallace*

CHAPTER 12

Never!

> **I will not retire while I've still got my legs and my make-up box.**
> — *Bette Davis*

Retire, I must not. Much wisdom I have yet to share.

— *Yoda, Star Wars: Episode II – Attack of the Clones*

Retiring is just practicing up to be dead. That doesn't take any practice.

— *Paul Harvey*

I always say, "Don't retire - inspire."

— *Mickey Rooney*

People who refuse to rest honorably on their laurels when they reach retirement age seem very admirable to me.

– *Helen Hayes*

My retiring days are behind me – they're going to have to throw me out now.

– *Garth Brooks*

Retire? I'm going to stay in show business until I'm the only one left.

– *George Burns*

Can someone really retire if he is passionate about what he does?

– *Hector Garcia Puigcerver, Ikigai: The Japanese Secret to a Long and Happy Life (2018)*

I'm still a horse that can run. I may not be able to win the Derby, but what do you do when you retire? People retire and they vegetate. They go away and they dry up.

– *Mel Brooks*

I love discomfort. I mean, my whole life is discomfort. One reason I can never retire is that the idea of just sitting on the beach totally comfortable is not a desideratum in my life. I like ambiguity, I like conflict, I like uncertainly.

– *Alan Dershowitz*

People think retiring is fun. Well, maybe. But if you have a certain kind of fire inside, there is no end in sight.

– *Sylvester Stallone*

The real boss in the family is my wife. She didn't want me hanging around the house all day and said, "You don't want to retire; you'll regret it." So, I listened to her.

– *Bill Gross*

I guess I don't really believe in retirement. I believe in shorter days and maybe in weekends!

– *Alice Waters*

"Retirement" is a dirty word. Luckily, I can carry on working until I drop, provided I retain my mental abilities.

– *Leslie Bricusse*

He can't understand people who long to retire. How can anyone spend their whole life longing for the day when they become superfluous?

— *Fredrik Backman, A Man Called Ove (2012)*

I have no intention of retiring. Even my blood sugar is better when I'm working.

— *Elaine Stritch*

I have no plans to retire. It's the perfect combination of work and play that keeps you young. If I quit work, it would be the beginning of the end for me.

— *Hugh Hefner*

I've never entertained the idea of retiring because I've never regarded myself as having a proper job. Anyway, retirement can be the death of you.

— *June Brown*

Why should I retire? I'm like a fighter. The bell rings, and you come out and fight.

— *Don Rickles*

I'll never retire. I like what I'm doing.

— *John Paul DeJoria*

He who wants to do more than he is able must admit defeat or retire.

– *Chrétien de Troyes, Arthurian Romances (1181)*

If I hear the word "retire," it makes me want to throw up. And then do what? Sit around all day watching television?

– *Joan Collins*

I will never retire unless I have to.

– *Dolly Parton*

Society tells you that when you're old you have to retire. You have to defy that.

– *Yoko Ono*

Retirement is fatal. Luckily, in my profession, you don't have to retire.

– *Joan Hickson*

It is a characteristic of potentates that they don't succumb to peaceful retirement. Instead, they hold power in their hoary fists as judgment and grip weaken, destroying any successors except family members.

– *Simon Sebag Montefiore*

There's nothing I would retire for, so I won't retire.

— *James Earl Jones*

I'm against retiring. The thing that keeps a man alive is having something to do.

— *Colonel Sanders*

People are always asking me when I'm going to retire. Why should I? I've got it two ways. I'm still making movies, and I'm a senior citizen, so I can see myself at half price.

— *George Burns*

I can't retire. My readers won't let me.

— *Clive Cussler*

When I do retire, you won't see me in the ring, but I will be working in the back with the young guys.

— *Mark Henry*

Just keep learning, keep changing and keep growing and promise me that you will never retire.

— *Neil Pasricha, The Happiness Equation: Want Nothing + Do Anything = Have Everything (2015)*

I love my fans. I love my music - I have no reason to retire.

— *LL Cool J*

Nothing is more bothersome to me than retiring. Weird things happen when you disengage; first you get negative, then you start telling people about your latest surgeries, and eventually you lose touch. I want to stay in touch.

— *Charles R. Swindoll*

I'm always announcing my retirement. I'm still not retired.

— *Dick Van Dyke*

I never use that word, retire.

— *B.B. King*

Let me put it this way: I don't plan to retire. What would I do, become a brain surgeon? I mean, a brain surgeon can retire and write novels, but a novelist can't retire and do brain surgery - or at least he better not.

— *Alan Furst*

And as long as people want to hear me sing, I don't know why I'd retire.

— *Tanya Tucker*

But intelligence officers never really retire, they just slip into the shadows.

— *Steig Larsson*

As long as I'm still able to have a hit on the radio and sell a few albums and some tickets, I don't see that it would be worth retiring.

— *Alan Jackson*

I love being Dr. Ruth, so I have never thought of retiring.

— *Ruth Westheimer*

Retirement has never, ever crossed my mind. And I honestly can't imagine when or why it would. If you're doing the thing you love, why on earth would you want to stop doing it?

— *Deborah Meaden*

I'm not ever going to retire. That's - that wouldn't be good, for one, just to go somewhere and sit down and do nothing. Please. No, that's not moi.

— *Aretha Franklin*

As my wife says, I'll never fully retire, but it'll start to slow down. I'll continue to do the local gigs or go to Las Vegas. But I won't be going out to Ohio to play an Indian casino anymore. Those will probably go by the wayside.

    – Bill Engvall

I retire every time I'm done with a movie. Then I go back. You know, I enjoy sleep. But I love to work; it's fun for me. As long as it continues to be fun, and I'm tolerated by the people around me, I will do it.

    – Harrison Ford

Retire? I don't know what that word means. As long as a man is able to work and he's productive out there and he feels good - keep at it.

    – Red Adair

I'll never retire. I'm just using up someone else's oxygen if I retire.

    – Sam Phillips

Sometimes I think about retiring, but not stopping work. Just "re-tir-ing" – put on some new tires and go on to do something else.

    – Jeff Bridges

Why should I say I will retire in three or four years? You retire the very moment you utter those words.

— *Haile Gebrselassie*

My wife asked me if I ever thought I would ever retire from stand-up. And I thought about it, and I was like, "No, because it's my job; it's what I do, and I enjoy it." It's still the most challenging thing for me to do.

— *Wanda Sykes*

Retirement is not in my vocabulary. They aren't going to get rid of me that way.

— *Betty White*

Saying, "I'm going to hang up my hat today, and I'm retiring," it's not a concept for me, and it never has been. I figure when I'm 81, I'll play 81-year-old parts. Hopefully.

— *William Fichtner*

Goodbye not because I'm retiring, but because I'm merely changing jobs. From being left tackle to being the number one fan of the Cleveland Browns.

— *Joe Thomas*

I wouldn't know what to do retiring. So, I have no plans to retire.

— *Ronald Meyer*

I don't see myself ever retiring, unless it's for something that I like better. And so far I like directing a lot, but I don't see the necessity to retire from anything unless there's a really great alternative.

— *Anjelica Huston*

My retirement date, every time you ask me that, I'm going to say five years. I don't want to retire.

— *Jamie Dimon*

Every time I try to retire, or even think of retiring from acting, my agent comes up with a script.

— *Anthony Hopkins*

I don't ever see myself retiring totally from music because I have a genuine love and passion for it.

— *Dr. Dre*

I don't believe in retiring. Your mind stops working then.

— *Lorne Greene*

If you really want to annoy me, ask me when I'm going to retire from rock n' roll.

– *Bruce Dickinson*

I'm not retiring. I am graduating. Today is my graduation day. Retirement means that you'll just go ahead and live on your laurels and surf all day in Oceanside. It ain't going to happen.

– *Junior Seau*

I'm not retiring because when you retire, you're still getting paid. I'm not getting paid, so I'm not retiring.

– *Vitor Belfort*

I don't want to retire. I still want to play.

– *Peyton Manning*

Sure, I've thought about retiring. But in my mind if you can't sing the song anymore, change the song and sing a different one!

– *Johnny Mathis*

When you do something that you like and you think you can keep doing it, you don't think about retiring.

– *Carolina Herrera*

I have no intention of retiring; I can't imagine not doing stand-up. That's where I started and where I'll be.

— *Bob Newhart*

I just don't see myself as retiring. As long as I'm healthy and can play the drums, that's what I'm going to do because that's the most fun thing that I know how to do.

— *Bill Kreutzmann*

CHAPTER 13

Showbiz

> **Musicians don't retire; they stop when
> there's no more music in them.**
> — *Louis Armstrong*

Actors can't retire. If actors retired, there would be nobody left to play old, wrinkly people. You have to keep going, darling - don't you?

— *Charles Dance*

I would look at older blues musicians who just keep going into their seventies. They keep doing it until they drop dead. And I've always felt like that's what I want to do. I've felt that since the day I was able to start playing music for a living. I don't see the point of thinking about retiring because it's not work to begin with.

— *Chris Cornell*

Actors never retire, they just get less and less work.

— *Desmond Llewelyn*

Old cartoonists never retire, they just erase away.

— *Mort Walker*

I haven't yet started to think about retiring. I was shocked when I heard Paul Newman retiring at age 82. Most actors just fade away like old soldiers.

— *Al Pacino*

Writers don't retire. I will always be a writer.

— *Andy Rooney*

Actors don't retire; people who are in jobs they don't like retire.

— *Bea Arthur*

Photography is not something you retire from.

— *Annie Leibovitz*

Baseball is going to end someday. I realize that as soon as you retire you know, people forget about you in this game fast! There's the next young guy coming up that's always better than you. So, for me, it's just about using baseball as a platform to do a lot of things.

— *Clayton Kershaw*

Art is one of the few careers without a mandatory retirement age.

    — *Julia Cameron*

Writers really don't retire, you know. They have to be taken out and shot.

    — *James Salter*

Retirement is purgatory for the former sports star. The world outside organized sports is unforgiving.

    — *John Gregory Dunne*

There's this idea of bankers retiring and painting watercolors. You can't dabble in art — it's a life. Being a writer, an artist... is a whole life.

    — *Justin Cartwright*

You don't quit in sports. You retire. You don't get to quit. It's not an option.

    — *Herm Edwards*

I think if you retire from touring, then people think you are retired.

    — *Alan Jackson*

The great thing about show business is that there's no mandatory retirement age.

    — *Scott Bakula*

CHAPTER 14

Miscellaneous

> **Not all treasure is made of silver and gold, mate.**
> **Retirement could very well be one of their treasures.**
> – *Captain Jack Sparrow, Pirates of the Caribbean:*
> *The Curse of the Black Pearl (2003)*

Middle class dreams of having enough money to retire. World class dreams of having enough money to impact the world.

    – *Steve Siebold, How Rich People Think (2010)*

You might be on the back nine of life, but it's good to finish strong.

    – *Morton Shaevitz, Refire! Don't Retire: Make the Rest of Your Life the Best of Your Life (2015)*

Hang in there, retirement is only thirty years away!

    – *Stephen Hawking*

I have said many times that most people work all their life to retire to play golf, while I played golf all my life to retire to work. I enjoy working. It has kept me young and on-the-move, and I have had a good time with it.

— *Jack Nicklaus*

Life is too short to wait until after retirement to live it.

— *Jason Zook, Own Your Weird: An Oddly Effective Way for Finding Happiness in Work, Life, and Love (2019)*

When you think about retiring, you're done. You already checked out.

— *Frank Gore*

I'd rather call it rewiring than retiring.

— *Russell Atkinson, Cached Out: A Cliff Knowles Mystery (2012)*

Why do we still work eight hours a day, 50 weeks a year, when we're twice as productive as we were 50 years ago?

— *Jacob Lund Fisker, Early Retirement Extreme: A philosophical and practical guide to finance independence (2010)*

Retirement isn't what it used to be. It used to be you retired and you disappeared off the face of the Earth. Now you have social media. I keep in touch with all my fans. It's great.

    – Anne Murray

One day blurs into the next, one week is indistinguishable from another. Their existence consists of waiting for the weekend, then waiting for retirement, and then waiting for death.

    – Marta Acosta, The She-Hulk Diaries (2013)

Real luxury is not working like a maniac to take an expensive vacation – it is living a life you enjoy every day.

    – Kathy Gottberg, RightSizing: A SMART Living 365 Guide to Reinventing Retirement (2016)

I don't understand the concept of retirement. It's not a bad thing to savor your memories, it can be wonderful and warming, but not at the cost of losing your excitement about the future.

    – William Shatner, Up Til Now (2008)

You get old faster when you think about retirement.

    – Toba Beta, Master of Stupidity (2011)

Retirement from job does not mean retirement from life! It is the beginning, not an end!

— *Ravi Samuel*

In the nineteenth century, there was no such thing as "retirement."

— *Thomas E. Woods, Jr., Real Dissent: A Libertarian Sets Fire to the Index Card of Allowable Opinion (2014)*

There's an enormous number of managers who have retired on the job.

— *Peter Drucker*

How much more dignified to retire from the world rather than wait for the world to tire of you.

— *Hugh Mahoney, Virgins & Martyrs (2012)*

A career may end with retirement and lots of "toys." A calling isn't over until the day you die.

— *John Ortberg, Jr., If You Want to Walk on Water, You've Got to Get Out of the Boat (2001)*

When you retire, people don't look at how good you became. They look at what you've won. We remember the winners.

— *Kylian Mbappe*

Retirement isn't a goal; it's a sentence.

– *Ari Gold*

In retirement, I look for days off from my days off.

– *Mason Cooley*

It took the Great Depression to make retirement into a reality in the United States. There were too many workers, too few jobs, and a consequent sense that the elderly needed to be nudged out of the labor pool.

– *Jessica Bruder, Nomadland: Surviving America in the Twenty-First Century (2017)*

As a subconscious attempt to add meaning or purpose to their life, the unemployed pray for a job; the retired pray for grandchildren.

– *Mokokoma Mokhonoana*

Your life is over when you stop living it. If you can truly retire you had a job, but not an occupation.

– *Roger Ebert, Life Itself: A Memoir (2012)*

Mr. S was finally retiring this year, which was a good thing, because he appeared to have run out of sh*ts to give sometime in the previous century.

— *Ernest Cline, Armada (2015)*

Sometimes it's hard to tell if retirement is a reward for a lifetime of hard work or a punishment.

— *Terri Guillemets*

Good memories are my retirement plan.

— *Atticus*

The key to retirement is to find joy in the little things.

— *Susan Miller*

Your best retirement plan for retiring happy and prosperous - don't be a burden on others.

— *Ernie J. Zelinski*

I have made noise enough in the world already, perhaps too much, and am now getting old, and want retirement.

— *French Emperor Napoleon Bonaparte*

Creativity doesn't retire.

— *Unknown*

A child born today is more likely to reach retirement age than his forebears were to live to their fifth birthday.

— *Johan Nordberg, Progress: Ten Reasons to Look Forward to the Future (2016)*

Spirit doesn't retire.

— *Toba Beta, My Ancestor Was an Ancient Astronaut (2010)*

For a few years after I stopped playing people would ask me how I was coping with retirement and there would often be a slightly worried tone to their voice. But I always answered the question the same way: that if I knew retirement was going to be this good, I would have quit a long time ago.

— *Tim Henman*

If anything could have pulled me out of retirement, it would have been an Indiana Jones film.

— *Sean Connery*

I want to go out in dramatic fashion. Win, lose, or draw, I want to have a retirement match, and a lot of guys have done it.

– Mark Henry

I'm not giving in to anyone else's idea of how I ought to feel and look at 70. "Retirement" is not a word I can even visualize. I retire when I go to bed!

– Carmen Dell'orefice

My career has been a positive one, and I want my retirement to be positive.

– John Havlicek

Once I retire, I'm retiring. I'm done.

– Michael Phelps

Retirement, we understand, is great if you are busy, rich, and healthy. But then, under those circumstances, work is great too.

– Bill Vaughan

I can't wait to be old and retired and say things just to see how people will react to get my kicks. That's the dream right there.

– Elsie Silver, Heartless (2022)

From the cradle to the grave, men are getting a raw deal. Men work longer hours, die earlier, but retire later than women.

— *British Parliament Member Dominic Raab*

Retirement is not a time to sleep, but a time to awaken to the beauty of the world around you and the joy that comes when you cast out all the negative elements that cause confusion and turmoil in your mind and allow serenity to prevail.

— *Howard Salzman*

Men in the uniform of Wall Street retirement: black Chesterfield coat, rimless glasses and the Times folded to the obituary page.

— *Jimmy Breslin*

People say people who spend too many years in prison don't know how to act when they get free. I don't know how I am going to act, how I am going to kill time, once I am not a fighter. Retirement scares me, and I have to think about how I am going to handle it.

— *Croatian Parliament Member Mirko Cro Cop*

If public servants are freely allowed to take up lucrative post-retirement jobs with companies to whom they have awarded contracts while they were in government, it would open up an easy way for companies to bribe public servants by offering them lucrative post-retirement jobs.

— *Prashant Bhushan*

I always likened retirement to falling off a cliff, and then you have to kind of brush yourself off.

— *Steve Young*

When I retire, everyone is going to respect me for fighting the big names.

— *Paulie Malignaggi*

I'm a Hall of Famer at retirement.

— *Carson Palmer*

One of the sad things about retiring is that you just become increasingly irrelevant. The world flows around you, and you don't seem to be impacting it any longer.

— *John Mackey*

Retire from your job, but never retire your mind.

— *Unknown*

Whereas in America we are so fearful of mortality, we don't want to talk about it, we don't think about it, and in many ways we treat elderly people as invisible because they are a constant reminder of our own mortality. We put them away and put them in retirement homes so we don't want to deal with that.

— *Lulu Wang*

When a band retires or is in hiding, a void is created. The fans' need is still there.

— *Billy Squier*

People are going to be living quite soon for 100 years. Our idea of how a family works no longer applies. It's no good saying you're going to have children for 15 years and then you're going to retire and have hobbies, because you've got 40 more years to go after 60 and you're in good health until 90 or something.

— *Theodore Zeldin*

It's not easy to retire. No one teaches you how. I found that out when I tried it the first time. I'm not a quitter.

— *Gordie Howe*

You can never have the comeback if you don't have the retirement.

— *Chael Sonnen*

A lot of people stop short. They don't actually die but they say, "Right I'm old, and I'm going to retire," and then they dwindle into nothing. They go off to Florida and become jolly boring.

— *Mary Wesley*

What's just about a generation of people who rack up government debt for their own health care and retirement - while leaving their children and grandchildren to foot the bill?

— *Rupert Murdoch*

For now, I'm building up stories for the retirement home!

— *Carol Vorderman*

Men are able to sustain a career into their 50s and 60s and still present themselves as sex symbols. With women, on the other hand, people say, "Why doesn't she retire?"

— *Tracy Chapman*

You are a person I really admire, because you are a person who gets to retire.

— *Unknown*

I'm not in retirement. I just don't want to work so much, and I don't get that many offers any more.

— *Max von Sydow*

Retirement is the perfect excuse to indulge in guilty pleasures without guilt; it's the sweet reward for a lifetime of hard work.

— *Mary Johnson, Retirement: The Grand Finale (2010)*

I made peace with retirement, but when you're a fighter, you're always a fighter.

— *Royce Gracie*

Retiring gives the impression that you're relieved that your job is over.

— *Michael Douglas*

People assume that they will retire at 60 and die when they are 70. If you can think positive, live a healthy life, listen to your body and follow a regime, then you can live for 100 years, healthy and happy.

— *Lok Sabha Member Hema Malini*

You can't retire from being great.

— *Unknown*

It's time to say goodbye, but I think goodbyes are sad, and I'd much rather say hello. Hello to a new adventure.

— *Ernie Harwell*

CONCLUSION

> **You can retire from a job, but don't ever retire from making extremely meaningful contributions in life.**
> — *Stephen R. Covey*

To summarize the above quotes, retirement:

1. represents change, which is both scary and exciting (be bold!),

2. brings freedom to do anything or nothing (your choice),

3. is a gift from God, so be grateful for this stage of life (not everyone gets this chance),

4. requires an adequate nest egg to fund the life you want (unless you enjoy the taste of government cheese), and

5. is an opportunity to commit to a new purpose (e.g., volunteer work, travel, quality time with family, gardening, etc.).

The differing perspectives and advice given on this topic are as numerous as the folks who call themselves retirees — which explains why it was relatively easy to find the 501 retirement quotes contained in this book.

The bottom line is that retirement is an adventure and a chance to do something meaningful with the rest of your life. In any case, I hope the quotes above made you laugh and perhaps think a little deeper about this important subject.

But wait, there's more! I saved the best for last. Below is the TOP TEN LIST of my all-time favorite retirement quotes.

10. A retired husband is often a wife's full-time job.

   — *Ella Harris*

9. Retirement is the perfect time to become the person you would have been if you weren't too busy being the person you had to be.

   — *Unknown*

8. There are some who start their retirement long before they stop working.

   — *Robert Half*

7. Before deciding to retire, stay home for a week and watch the day-time TV shows.

   — *Bill Copeland*

6. It is better to live rich than to die rich.

   — *Samuel Johnson*

5. I really think that it's better to retire, in Uncle Earl's terms, when you still have some snap left in your garters.

— *U.S. Senator Russell B. Long*

4. You know you're getting old when work is a lot less fun and fun is a lot more work.

— *Joan Rivers*

3. It can be tempting just to say, "Well, I'm going to retire." But what will you do then? Sit in a chair and watch TV? Don't let fulfillment throw away your tomorrow.

— *Robert H. Schuller*

2. Life is either a daring adventure or nothing at all. And retirement? It's the perfect time for daring.

— *Helen Keller*

And my number one all-time favorite retirement quote is...

1. How lucky I am to have something that makes saying goodbye so hard.

— *Winnie-the-Pooh*

Lastly, I'll close out this silly book with one final retirement quote for you to ponder:

> **Retirement is wonderful if you have two essentials — much to live on and much to live for.**
> — *Unknown*

LET'S GET CONNECTED

I hope you enjoyed this silly book! If so, **please do two small favors for me right now.**

First, please take a minute to leave a short review of this book on Amazon, Goodreads, or any other website. Online reviews help new readers find this book. Your help in spreading the word about this book is greatly appreciated!

Second, please sign up for my reader's list at www.mikekowis.com/ signup/ so that we can get connected. After you join, I'll occasionally share exclusive giveaways and announcements about my upcoming books and speaking engagements.

If you have any questions or wish to contact me about speaking to your group, I'm just an email away! Feel free to contact me anytime at mike.kowis.esq@gmail.com.

Happy Trails!

ACKNOWLEDGEMENTS

This book would not have been possible without the extraordinary help and support of many folks, including my dear family, friends, and fellow authors.

I also want to offer my sincere appreciation to my long-time friend and movie aficionado, Robert Ziggy Parker, for his generous help in refining the testimonials for this book. In case you didn't figure it out, I made them up for my readers' amusement. If you didn't enjoy them, I blame Mr. Parker! If you loved them, I want to thank you in advance and let you know that Ziggy played a big part in making these zingers as humorous as possible.

Last, I want to give special thanks to Robynne Alexander at Damonza for the cover design, interior print formatting, and eBook conversion work.

It takes a skillful and dedicated team to create a book like this, and everyone who participated has my sincere appreciation for their contributions.

ABOUT THE AUTHOR

By day, **Mike Kowis, Esq.**, is a mild-mannered tax attorney at a Fortune 500 company in Texas. By night, he swaps a three-piece suit for a pair of tights and a shiny red cape and then begins his duties as a modern-day SUPERHERO (also known as Adjunct Faculty Member) for one of the largest community colleges in the Lone Star State.

Specifically, Mike has practiced corporate tax law for 27 years, including the last quarter-century at Entergy Services, LLC where he currently serves as Senior Tax Counsel. In addition, he has taught corporate tax and business law classes at Lone Star College-Montgomery since 2001. In his spare time, he writes books and competes in off-road races.

Mike holds a bachelor's degree and two law degrees, including a LL.M. in taxation from Georgetown University Law Center. He lives in Texas with his family, and his award-winning books are listed below.

In his debut book, ***Engaging College Students: A Fun and Edgy Guide for Professors***, Mike shared the secrets to his success in the college classroom. Specifically, he provided 44 college teaching tips to help any teacher create a fun and lively learning environment, engage students in thought-provoking classroom discussions, motivate them to read the assigned materials, inspire them to attend all classes and stay till the final bell rings, and encourage them to use their critical thinking skills.

In his most popular book, *14 Steps to Self-Publishing a Book*, Mike explains how he turned the manuscript of his first book into a high-quality self-published book. This short and practical guide spells out 14 steps that anyone can follow to self-publish a top-quality book and sell it on websites like Amazon and BarnesandNoble.com. He also details the costs of his self-publishing journey and shares the top 10 lessons he learned from writing his first book.

In his first co-author project, Mike teamed up with seasoned author and book coach, Sharon C. Jenkins, to write a free eBook, *Maximize Your Book Sales With Data Analysis: The Cure for Authorship Analysis Paralysis*, which is intended to help self-published authors make the most of their book marketing efforts and tackle the dreaded authorship analysis paralysis.

In the following book, *Smart Marketing for Indie Authors: How I Sold my First 1,563 Books and Counting!*, Mike explains his proven book-selling formula and the 16 marketing tools he used to break 1,500 book sales within his first two years of being an independently-published author. Mike has used these same techniques to sell over 6,500 copies to date. He also provides the effectiveness rating for each marketing tactic along with the costs and time commitment involved.

During the pandemic, seasoned amateur competitor Mike Kowis launched *Texas Off-road Racing: A Father-Son Journey to a Side-by-Side Championship*, where he shares what off-road racing feels like from the driver's seat, plus how much money and time is required to compete in this harrowing motorsport. He also gives the gritty details of each side-by-side race that he and his teenage son competed in during their run for the 2019 Championship in a local off-road racing series. Whether you are a long-time off-road racer with 10 titles to your name, someone curious to learn about the sport, or a parent looking for exciting father-son activities, this book will surely entertain and enlighten you.

In his fifth book, ***American Tax Trivia: The Ultimate Quiz on U.S. Taxation***, Mike challenges readers to 250 fun-filled trivia questions about federal income taxation. (Eureka! Did he just say fun-filled and taxation in the same sentence?) Specifically, this book quizzes readers on the rich and sometimes stormy history of U.S. tax law, the Internal Revenue Code, and important case law. Additional topics include amusing tax quotes, the United States Treasury Department, the Internal Revenue Service, tax forms, audits, politics, plus odds and ends that don't neatly fit into the above categories. Whether you are a seasoned tax practitioner, a neophyte taxpayer looking for an overview of U.S. taxation, a history buff, or just a trivia junky looking for your next fix, you will surely enjoy testing your knowledge of American taxation.

Next, Mike launched ***Texas Off-road Racing 2: The Battle for ATV and Side-by-Side Championships*** as the long-awaited sequel to *Texas Off-road Racing: A Father-Son Journey to a Side-by-Side Championship*. Here, Mike shares the gritty details of each round of ATV and side-by-side racing during his run for the 2022 championships in a brand new off-road racing series in Texas. Whether you are an experienced off-road racer, a newbie to the sport, or a parent looking for exciting activities to enjoy with your child, this book will surely entertain and enlighten you.

In his next book entitled ***The Little Black Book of Tax Wisdom***: ***Quotes, Quips, & Quiddities Every Tax Advisor Should Know***, Mike presents the complete handbook of tax wisdom, past and present. This leisurely read contains a huge collection of amusing tax quotes from Mark Twain, Chris Rock, Ronald Reagan, Winston Churchill, George Washington, Judge Learned Hand, David Letterman, and many more. It is intended for students and tax advisors of all stripes, including certified public accountants, tax attorneys, IRS enrolled agents, and the like. This is the perfect complement to his other tax-related book, *American Tax Trivia: The Ultimate Quiz on U.S. Taxation.*

In this book, ***The Little Black Book of Retirement Wisdom: Amusing Quotes for Retirees***, Mike presents the complete handbook of retirement wisdom, past and present. This leisurely read contains a huge collection of amusing and thought-provoking retirement quotes from Betty White, Elon Musk, Mark Twain, Brett Favre, Joan Rivers, Dr. Dre, Billy Graham, George Foreman, and many more. It is intended for all retirees and anyone considering the "Big R."

If you have any questions or would like Mike to speak at an upcoming event, please email him at mike.kowis.esq@gmail.com, find his author page on Facebook (Mike Kowis, Esq.), or visit his website at www.mikekowis.com.

Made in the USA
Columbia, SC
10 June 2024